Artful Eggs

Artful Eggs

 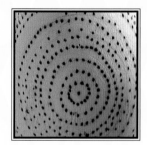  

Six Dozen Extraordinary Ways to Decorate an Egg

Terry Taylor

LARK BOOKS

A Division of
Sterling Publishing Co., Inc.
New York

Library of Congress Cataloging-in-Publication Data

Taylor, Terry, 1952-
    Artful eggs : six dozen extraordinary ways to decorate
an egg / by Terry Taylor.-- 1st ed.
        p. cm.
    Includes index.
    ISBN 1-57990-463-7 (hardcover)
    1. Egg decoration. 2. Eggshell craft. I. Title.
    TT896.7.T39 2004
    745.594'4--dc22
                                        2003015268

10 9 8 7 6 5 4 3 2 1

First Edition

Published by Lark Books,
a division of Sterling Publishing Co., Inc.
387 Park Avenue South, New York, N.Y. 10016

© 2004, Lark Books

Distributed in Canada by Sterling Publishing,
c/o Canadian Manda Group, One Atlantic Ave., Suite 105
Toronto, Ontario, Canada M6K 3E7

Distributed in the U.K. by Guild of Master Craftsman Publications Ltd.
Castle Place, 166 High Street, Lewes, East Sussex, England BN7 1XU
Tel: (+ 44) 1273 477374, Fax: (+ 44) 1273 478606,
Email: pubs@thegmcgroup.com, Web: www.gmcpublications.com

Distributed in Australia by Capricorn Link (Australia) Pty Ltd.
P.O. Box 704, Windsor, NSW 2756 Australia

If you have questions or comments about this book, please contact:
Lark Books
67 Broadway
Asheville, NC 28801
(828) 253-0467

Manufactured in China

ISBN 1-57990-463-7

Art Director
Kristi Pfeffer

Photo Stylist
Celia Naranjo

Principal Photographer
Sandra Stambaugh

Additional Photography
Evan Bracken, 65; Steve Mann, 123

Special Photography
Sanoma Syndication: D. Straatemeier, 90,
104,109; D. Brandsma, 2; R. Frinking, 107;
H. Zeegers, 7,112,113; R. Beck, 66;
P. Grotes, 108

Cover Designer
Barbara Zaretsky

Assistant Editor
Nathalie Mornu

Associate Art Director
Shannon Yokeley

Editorial Assistance
Delores Gosnell

CONTENTS

Introduction 6

The Basics 8

*Absolutely everything you need to know about
all kinds of eggs and preparing them for decorating.
Learn what simple tools you'll need, handy how-to
techniques, methods of coloring eggs, and hints for
presentation and display.*

The Projects 19

*Dozens of easy and imaginative ways to
decorate eggs. From brightly colored eggs adorned
with glittery stickers (oh, so simple!) to more challenging,
one-of-a-kind china mosaic eggs, you'll find a wide
range of projects to inspire you.*

Artful Eggs in and around the Home 105

*An elaborate springtime buffet, egg place cards,
altered art, wreaths, and—of course—egg trees.
These are just a few of the ideas for decorating with
eggs you'll discover in this chapter.*

Introduction

Eggs are one of nature's perfect shapes. They're symbols of creation, purity, fertility, and resurrection. They're the subject of myths and stories (remember Aesop's magical goose laying golden eggs or Sam-I-Am and his green eggs?). And in most cultures they're culinary staples, from eggs Benedict to China's 1,000 year-old eggs.

But why decorate eggs? Well, why not? They're irresistible blank canvases. They take on color well, have smooth surfaces, and their shape—though it's elegant even when unadorned—invites something more.

With the simplest of crafting techniques you can create an amazing variety of decorated eggs. I've assembled a team of talented designers to help me show you how. We've created projects using everything from ordinary chicken eggs and delicate quail eggs to ostrich eggs, papier mâché eggs, and even those brilliantly colorful plastic eggs that fill the stores each spring. The techniques we use are easy and familiar. If you can cut, paste, paint, or count to 20 (for bead netting) you can transform an egg into something artful. We'll show you how to decorate eggs with natural leaf stencils and dyes, how to paint charming chicks, how to gild, etch, and adorn eggs with everything from tissue paper and millinery trim to polymer clay and photo transfers.

In addition to projects, you'll find dozens of ideas for displaying your very own artful eggs all year round. Show off a basket filled with outsized red and gold eggs during the winter holidays. Make your Easter morning buffet a memorable occasion with a simple centerpiece of eggs and flowers. A collection of speckled bird eggs can be far more than a simple science project—it can be artful.

With this book in hand you have no *egg-cuzes* not to decorate a dozen *eggs-traordinary* and *el-egg-ant* eggs.

The Basics

An Egg-Cylcopedia

You have dozens of questions about eggs that you're dying to ask, don't you? Here are the answers to some of them.

Q: *What are the largest or smallest eggs?*

A: The smallest bird egg is the hummingbird's (less than 1/2 inch or 1 cm), and the largest egg (from 6 to 9 inches or 15 to 23 cm) is laid by the ostrich. Man-made eggs can be any size.

Q: *Why are eggshells different colors?*

A: Egg color is not influenced by what the bird eats, but by genetics. Chickens with white earlobes (really!) lay white eggs; reddish-lobed chickens lay eggs that range in color from light tan to dark brown. Never mind why robins lay blue eggs or Aracuna hens, green ones. Chalk it up to genetics.

Q: *What kinds of eggs can you decorate?*

A: Here's the rule: If the egg is domestically raised (and that includes ostrich and emu) or if it's a factory-made egg, you can decorate any and all of them at will. If you plan on robbing a robin's or wren's nest for an egg to decorate, shame on you. Wild bird eggs are off limits. Never remove them from their nests no matter how tempting they are. If you're lucky, you might find a delightfully blue robin's egg that rolled out of the nest laying in the grass. Don't decorate it—treasure it.

Chicken Eggs

Chicken eggs are classified into six sizes based on weight. You'll find jumbo, extra large, large, and medium eggs in most grocery stores. Two additional sizes—small and peewee—round out the classification. Chicken eggs range in color from white to brown except for the lovely eggs of the small, hybrid Aracuna species. These jewels of the domestic fowl family range in color from the palest green to olive or turquoise.

Other Domestic Fowl

Goose eggs are more elongated than chicken eggs and have very white, smooth shells. They're twice the size of jumbo hen's eggs. If you don't have a gaggle in your yard, you can purchase goose eggs from online sources. Domestic duck eggs range in color from white to a pale blue. They're more oval than goose eggs and slightly smaller.

Some species of quail are raised domestically. Their shells are very thin and fragile, and they're just short of an inch (2.54 cm) tall. Pure white eggs are from bobwhite quails; brownish-speckled eggs are from cotournix breeds. Blow them with care.

Giants of the Egg World

The ostrich produces a very thick, strong-shelled egg. So strong they almost feel like ceramic if you flick them with your fingernail or heft one in the palm of your hand. The surface of the shell is pitted and ivory colored.

A cousin to the ostrich, the emu produces a large egg that ranges in color from dark emerald green to nearly black. The egg has a heavily textured outer shell. It's favored by some egg crafters for etching and scraffito techniques because the outer shell carves away to reveal a lighter-colored layer of shell.

Man-Made Eggs

Turned on lathes, wooden eggs come in a

variety of shapes and sizes from wren sized to goose sized. They're great for decorative painting, gilding, wood burning, and carving. You'll find them with the wood products in your local craft store year round.

Papier mâché eggs are available most of the year as well. The larger the egg, the more likely it is to have a plastic inner layer covered with brown kraft paper. These eggs are great canvases for decoupage and painting techniques.

Polystyrene foam eggs come in a variety of sizes. You can use them as a form for your own papier mâché eggs or as a base for mosaic eggs.

When the Easter seasonal displays appear in stores you'll find a wide assortment of colorful plastic eggs. These eggs are made in one or two pieces ranging in size from hummingbird-like to something so big, you definitely don't want to see its mother flying over your head.

In addition, you can purchase ceramic greenware eggs to paint and fire; clear glass ornaments you can paint with glass paints; and egg-shape boxes. If you have garden space, you can even raise your own egg-shape gourds.

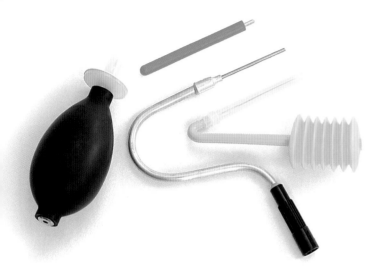

Preparing Eggs for Decoration

There are two methods used to prepare natural eggs before you decorate them— blowing out the contents or cooking the contents. For either method, the first thing you want to do is examine your eggs for any visible cracks in the shells. The eggshell should feel dry to the touch. A noticeably slimy feeling may indicate bacterial growth, and powdery spots that come off when touched may indicate mold. Discard these eggs.

How to Blow Out an Egg

Blowing out the contents of an egg is an excellent way to insure that your olafactory senses won't be unpleasantly surprised when you unpack your decorated eggs. If you're planning on decorating large quantities (more than a dozen) of eggs, take it from

one who knows, investing in egg-blowing tools is a good idea. Depending on the type of tool you purchase, you pierce one end of the egg with a needle or special drill, and blow into a pipe or squeeze a pump to force the contents out of the egg into a container. Simple enough.

If you don't have the specialized tools for blowing an egg, wash the egg with a very mild solution of bleach and water, and dry it well. Pierce each end of the egg with a large needle. Place your lips on one end (that's why you washed the egg). Unless you want to end up with the proverbial you-know-what on your face and clothes, gently blow the contents into a bowl. If the eggs are fresh and you don't have a cold, you can whip up a flan for dessert, serve a fritatta for dinner, or relax for a few minutes with a simple facial mask made of one beaten egg combined with a small spoonful of honey.

No matter how you blow it, it's also important to clean out the inside of your blown egg. Fill a syringe with warm, soapy water. Inject the solution into the egg and shake it gently while covering the hole(s) with your finger(s). Blow or shake out the contents and place the egg on a drying rack to drain and dry thoroughly.

How to Hard-cook an Egg

If you don't want to blow out your egg's contents, here's how to make the perfect hard-cooked egg, which you can devil, chop up for egg salad, or decorate for an Easter morning game of hide-and-seek.

For decorating, the most crucial aspect of boiling an egg is doing so without cracking the shell. Inspect each egg carefully for hairline cracks before beginning. Immerse refrigerated eggs in hot tap water for approximately five minutes before cooking them. Extreme changes in temperature can stress the shell and make it crack. Some sources recommend piercing the shell with a pin. In theory this allows air to escape and prevents pressure from building up inside and cracking the egg from the inside out. It's not absolutely necessary, however.

To cook them, place the eggs (which have been warmed in hot tap water) in a lidded, heavy saucepan that is large enough to hold them in a single layer. Cover them with cold tap water (and add a pinch of salt if you plan to peel them later). Partially cover the pan with the lid and heat on high until the water comes to a full boil. Turn down the heat and count slowly to 30 before taking the pot off the burner. Let the eggs stand in the hot water, tightly covered, for 15 minutes. Gently pour off most of the hot water, place the eggs in a colander, and rinse them under cold running water for five minutes. When cooled, wipe them dry with a clean cloth.

Eggs should be refrigerated immediately after cooking and cooling. Cooked eggs left at room temperature for more than two hours, including the preparation time, or for more than 30 minutes when the temperature is 85° F (63°C) or more, cannot be considered safe for consumption. Cooked eggs can be refrigerated in their cartons and should be placed in the coldest part of the refrigerator (not the door) where the temperature is at least 40° F (8°C) or less. Hard-cooked eggs will keep in the refrigerator for one week.

If you plan to decorate the hard-cooked eggs—and forbid anyone to eat a single one of them—apply a couple of coats of acrylic varnish to seal them before you begin to decorate. If you hide decorated hard-cooked eggs for Easter, it's best not to eat them later. The wisest course is to decorate a set of eggs for hiding and set aside a dozen hard-cooked eggs for eating.

Tools

Before you start decorating, gather up an egg basket of basic craft tools. Each set of project directions assumes that you have these tools, then lists the specific materials needed to create that particular project. If a special type of glue is recommended for example, it will be listed. The basic craft tools in your egg basket won't be repeated each and every time.

A Tisket, A Tasket
(What You Need In Your Basket)

You probably have them on hand anyway, but here are the tools you should have in your basket.

- *A pencil and paper for making templates or preliminary sketches*

- *Your favorite pair(s) of scissors*

- *A measuring tape, or ruler and string (see page 16)*

- *White craft glue, a hot glue gun and glue sticks, and cellophane tape*

- *Darning or tapestry needles (essential for piercing eggs)*

- *Paintbrushes: large and small, broad and fine tipped*

- *Undyed wooden toothpicks (handy for placing dabs of glue where you want them)*

- *Bamboo skewers*

- *Plastic kitchen wrap (see page 18)*

Other Handy Tools

Each of the following tools can be added to your egg basket of essential tools. You'll find them useful for all sorts of crafting projects. And who doesn't need more tools?

Bone folders are great for burnishing glued things and smoothing out wrinkles in tape or paper. If you don't have a bone folder, a simple craft stick will work in a pinch.

Hand-held, motorized cutting tools are wonderful modern inventions. Use them to drill holes, cut things apart, and to sand.

A **craft lathe** is perfect if you need both hands free, or want to paint a continuous line around an egg. You can find these light-duty tools in craft stores or online sites that specialize in egg craft or pysanky. In a pinch, you can also simply place a blown egg on a bamboo skewer. Stand the skewer in a piece of polystyrene foam if you need to use two hands, or hold the skewer in one hand as you decorate the egg with the other.

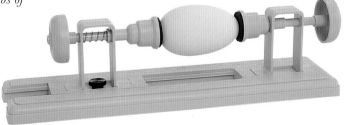

A **Kistky** or a **tjanting** are tools you'll need for batik and other resist work. Use them to apply melted beeswax to a surface. Ukrainian *pysanky* makers use many types of *kistky*, electric or heated with a small flame; traditional batik dyers use a *tjanting*. Each of these tools is basically a small funnel attached to a stick. Wax is placed in the funnel, heated, and the tool is drawn across the surface, creating a wax line.

Dryer racks solve the pesky problem of what to do with freshly dyed or cleaned, but wet, eggs. Setting down a wet, dyed egg on a flat surface leaves a large, unsightly spot on the shell when it dries; a blown and cleaned egg needs to drain and dry before you use it. Make a rack with a piece of hard polystyrene foam and some bamboo skewers, short lengths of coat hanger wire, or even toothpicks inserted into the foam. Slip blown eggs onto the skewers, or prop dyed eggs on

a trio of toothpicks, and they'll dry or drain overnight. You can also use the rack to hold eggs in place when you use aerosol paints or varnishes.

A **doll needle** is just the thing you need to thread ribbon through eggs. The length of the needle makes it easy to run the needle through all but the largest of eggs, and its large eye is easy to thread.

Rubber or latex gloves protect your hands when you're dyeing eggs. It's a fact of life: If you don't want to walk around with blue or green fingers keep a stash of gloves handy.

Nonreactive pans are nice to have when you are dyeing eggs. Some dyes react when they come in contact with metal pans and may change color.

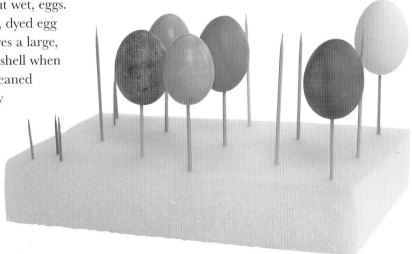

Enamel-coated or glass pans are best. If you plan to do a lot of dyeing, it's wise to purchase a pan and reserve it solely for dyes.

Slotted plastic serving spoons are perfect for lifting eggs from a dye bath. Don't try to use those small, disposable picnic spoons; they won't give your egg enough support on its trip from the dye bath to the drying rack. You can guess what might happen.

Syringes (without needles!) are great tools for injecting soapy water into a blown egg for a final cleaning. You can also inject dye inside a blown egg (see page 60). Save those syringes you brought home from a visit to the veterinarian; they'll come in handy.

Coloring Eggs

Natural eggshells have porous surfaces with individual characteristics just like human skin. Some are more porous than others, some lighter or darker. Dyeing an eggshell isn't an exact science and won't be a completely predictable process. Even eggs from the same carton (goodness knows that doesn't mean they're from the same hen!) have different shell characteristics and will absorb dye at different rates.

In general, it's best to mix up fresh batches of dye when you want to color eggs. Using distilled water and nonreactive pans takes some of the variance out of the dyeing process. Dyes subtly react with chemicals in tap water and to certain metals in cookware.

You'll obtain the best dye coverage when you dye unblown or hard-cooked eggs; they sink in the dye bath, while blown eggs tend to float. You'll have to hold a blown egg under the surface until the dye bath fills the inside of the egg. Allow the dyed egg to dry completely, then blow the contents if it's not hard-cooked.

Food Coloring

These simple dyes are found crammed way in the back of most kitchen cabinets. They're the basis of many childhood memories. More than one person has remarked that the smell of warm vinegar brings to mind dyeing Easter eggs as a child.

Food coloring dyes come in liquid or paste forms and are food safe. You can color hard-cooked eggs with them, and rest assured that you can safely peel the egg and eat it. Like many dye baths, they're best used when hot, and usually require a mordant of vinegar to fix the color.

Natural Dyes

Creating your own easy-to-use natural dyes is a fun experiment. Part of their charm is the variety of tone and shade you get with each batch of dyestuff. If you're not open to chance and the subtle variety of its effects, stick to more reliable synthetic dyes. If you're adventurous, you'll be amply rewarded with the subtle coloring of natural dyes.

There aren't many hard-and-fast rules or recipes for working with natural dyestuffs from your kitchen. Just be sure you add a teaspoon of vinegar to any concoction you create from natural materials to act as a mordant for your dye. The more natural material you use, the more intense the color will be. And, for best results, be sure to use your dye while it's lukewarm. If you leave your eggs in the dye bath overnight, you'll achieve the darkest color possible with your natural materials.

Boiled onion skins are a common natural dyestuff and a good place to start. Save a hefty handful of brown or red onion skins, bring them to a boil in a small pan of water with a teaspoon of vinegar, and simmer them for 10 minutes. This recipe will dye your eggs a pleasing orange-brown color.

Beet skins, as any cook knows, will turn anything red (including your hands!). Chopped cranberries will create a pleasant, pale pink. Shredded red cabbage leaves or canned blueberries will make soothing shades of blue. Ground turmeric from your spice rack will make a nice yellow, as will ground cumin or celery seed. Chop some spinach leaves for a pale green. Brewed coffee and teas will also color your eggs. Experiment with carrot tops and discover what color your dyed eggs will be. That's half the fun.

Other more traditional natural dyes—indigo, madder, cochineal, or logwood—can be purchased from stores that supply dyes to yarn spinners and weavers. The effects of these dyes are more predictable than the kitchen stove method described above. Use the manufacturer's recommended mordants for best results.

Synthetic Dyes

Follow the manufacturer's instructions for using these dyes. Their final effect is usually reliable, even given the vagaries of dyeing an egg. Since these dyes are chemically created, they should never be used to color eggs that are going to be eaten.

Paints

For a really predictable color, paint your eggs with acrylic paint. It's easy to work with and dries quickly. One drawback to using an acrylic paint is that it sits on the surface and looks like a coat of paint. This may not be desirable on natural eggs, but isn't necessarily a bad thing when you use it on wood, paper, or plastic egg shapes.

Gouaches—matte, opaque watercolor paints mixed with a preparation of gum—closely approximate the subtle matte finish of a natural eggshell. Several of the projects in this book were painted with gouache.

Never eat hard-cooked eggs that are painted with acrylics or gouaches.

Other Coloring Agents

Use colored pencils or markers to draw simple designs or to add accent colors to your dyed eggs. Crayons can be used to color eggs and also as a simple form of wax resist. Draw or write on the egg with a white crayon, slip the egg into a dye bath and—voila!—you've created a variation of a batik egg (see page 72).

How-To Techniques

The techniques used in this book for decorating eggs probably will be familiar to almost every crafter. If not, they can be easily learned. Embellishing eggs with simple materials—craft foam, thread, and tissue paper—doesn't require special expertise. Even the more complex techniques such as batik, bead netting, or mosaic work are easy enough to accomplish. And even if you can't draw a straight line, you can re-create the delightful peeps (page 40) or bunnies (page 82) by following the step-by-step directions.

Allow yourself some creative leeway; your eggs shouldn't look exactly like the projects pictured. You won't have any fun if you're worried that your blue isn't the same shade or that your ribbon is wider than the one pictured. Decorating eggs should be fun, frivolous, and maybe even slightly egg-centric.

Here are four handy how-to techniques that everyone should know before they decorate an egg.

How to Measure an Egg

If you want to know how much ribbon to buy to wrap around a dozen eggs, you'll need to know the circumference of an egg. That's easy enough to figure out: Wrap a measuring tape around the widest part or around the length of the egg. If you don't have a measuring tape, wrap a length of string around the egg and measure it with a ruler.

How to Cover an Egg

If you're covering an egg with paper (see page 68), simply create a rectangle with two measurements. First, measure around the widest part of the egg. Then measure around the length of the egg and divide this measurement in half. A rectangle created with these two measurements gives you more than enough paper to completely cover the egg.

To smoothly and almost seamlessly cover the egg, follow these directions:

1. On the "wrong" side of the paper rectangle, mark the paper into thirds along the long length with a pencil.
2. Evenly divide and mark the rectangle into small vertical strips. The width of your strips will be determined by the size of the egg you're covering. A hen's egg will require smaller strips than, say, an ostrich or large plastic egg.
3. Cut all of the strips up to—but not through—the center section. Trim the ends of each strip into small, curved points.
4. Cut off an entire section of three strips. Glue it to your egg, easing the strips into place and overlapping them, if needed. Cut off the next section and glue it into place right next to the first section. Don't be tempted to cut all of the sections at once. Cut and glue them one at a time.

Guest Designer: Lynne Krucke

How to Divide an Egg

You may wish to evenly divide your egg into quadrants. Doing so can become a design element (by coloring the quadrants different colors) or may help you place design elements equally around the egg.

Draw a light pencil line vertically from the center of the top to the center of the bottom. Turn the egg 180 degrees, and repeat. Then draw a line horizontally around the widest part of the egg. You will have four quadrants. You can further divide the sections into smaller sizes. In addition, you can draw diagonal lines starting from the point where two lines cross.

How to Glue Almost Anything to an Egg

When you glue one thing to another, you often need to press the two together until the glue dries. Sometimes you might even use a heavy book to hold them together. I haven't tried it, but I don't think this method will work with an egg.

If you need to hold and press something to an egg until the glue dries, you'll need a square of plastic wrap. Place the egg in the center of the plastic wrap. Gather the corners and twist them together, pulling the wrap and the glued embellishment tightly against the egg—but not too tightly or you-know-what will happen! Loosen the wrap when you think the glue has had time to dry.

Presentation

Once you've blown, dyed, and decorated a dozen eggs, what will you do with them? Give them to someone, or display them in your own home? You could nestle a dozen in a pretty basket filled with artificial grass, but that's a pat solution, and you've worked so hard. Why not make your presentation as imaginative as your eggs?

Baskets are a traditional choice for displaying eggs, but don't limit yourself to the usual styles or sizes. Miniature baskets—wire, wood, glass, or plastic—are great showcases for single eggs. An oversize decorative basket filled with one or a dozen eggs can become the decorative focal point in a room (page 121). Bowls and platters, decorative bags and boxes, even the humble egg carton (page 54), can all be utilized for creative display and presentation.

A single, artful egg demands its very own pedestal. Plus it won't stand upright without one. Egg cups are the obvious choice for displaying eggs. If you don't have china or glass egg cups in your kitchen cabinet, you'll find them in kitchen stores, antique shops, or even in the wood products section of your local craft store. Small plastic curtain rings give the rounded end of an egg just enough support to stand upright almost invisibly; if you're looking to make more of a statement, use a napkin ring (page 52).

Have as much fun choosing what to use for presentation as you did in deciding how to decorate your artful eggs.

Artful Egg Projects

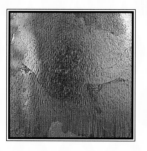

Fauxaics

Foe-zay-iks. Clever name for a clever technique.
They don't come much easier than this one.

- Gouaches
- Pencil
- Clear acrylic fixative

1. Hold an egg between your middle finger and thumb (or use a craft lathe) while decorating it.
2. Gouache paints are opaque, matte colors that dry very quickly. Apply them liberally to each egg as a basecoat. Let the basecoat dry.
3. When the paint is dry, hold an egg in the palm of your hand and paint each end. Allow paint to dry.
4. Use a sharp pencil to lightly sketch mosaic designs created with small squares, triangles, or other geometric shapes onto eggs. Paint the sketched designs. After the paint dries, outline the designs with a soft pencil or colored pencil.
5. Spray the finished eggs with fixative.

Guest Designer: Lynne Caldwell

Nature's Stencils

Nature's shapes and natural dyes are the perfect complements to one of nature's most elegant forms.

- Whole eggs
- Natural dyes*
- Small leaves, fronds and flowers
- Nylon stockings
- Small rubber bands

*See page 15 for a basic description of some natural dyes. Lynnes used cochineal, brazilwood, logwood, and osage, with alum as the mordant.

Prepare the natural dyes ahead of time, giving them time to cool before submerging eggs.

1. Use unblown eggs for this project so they will sink in the dye bath and color evenly.

2. Prepare the natural dyes ahead of time, giving them time to cool before submerging eggs.

3. Take a stroll in your yard or a park and look for small leaves or flowers. Pansies, fern fronds, and Japanese maple leaves all work well, as do four-leaf clovers if you're lucky enough to find one.

4. Place a leaf on an egg. Carefully wrap the egg inside a single layer of nylon stocking material. Pull it tight against the egg. Tie the loose ends or secure them with small rubber bands on the side opposite the leaf.

5. Submerge the egg in the dye bath until the desired color is achieved. Five or 10 minutes should be enough time.

6. Remove the egg from the dye and allow it to dry before you remove the stocking. Remove the stocking and the leaf.

7. You can repeat this process to add additional designs and colors on the egg if desired. Just remember to start with the lightest color first, followed by the darker colors.

8. If desired, follow the instructions on page 10 for blowing an egg.

Guest Designer: Lynne Caldwell   Artful Eggs   23

Desert Sunrise Pastels

You wouldn't want sand in your eggs, but you can use sand on them to create a subtle matte surface. To achieve a totally different, glitzy effect, substitute fine glitter or micro-beads. Then you can call them Las Vegas Sunset Eggs.

- Double-sided adhesive tape
- Craft sand in assorted colors
- Clear matte acrylic spray varnish

1. Wrap the tape onto the egg in the pattern you want for the first color. Sprinkle the sand over the egg. Shake off excess sand.

2. Wrap the tape onto the egg for a second color. Sprinkle the color over the egg and shake off the excess sand. Repeat as desired.

3. Spray egg with clear varnish.

Guest Designer: Joan Morris

Jungle Fever

Oh, the mind boggling animals these eggs might produce. Thank goodness they won't hatch!

- Papier mâché eggs*
- Animal print napkins
- Decoupage medium

Joan used papier mâché eggs. You can use whatever type of egg you wish.

1. Separate the napkin layers. You'll use only the top printed layer.
2. Tear or cut the printed layers into strips.
3. Coat a small area of the egg with decoupage medium.
4. Lay the napkin onto the egg, tapping it into place with your fingers. Take care not to smear and tear the napkin. Continue to cover the egg, alternating the animal prints. If you wish, you can create a plain zebra, tiger, or leopard egg.
5. Work on half of an egg at a time. Allow it dry while you work on another egg. Finish covering the egg when it feels dry.
6. Give each egg a final coat of decoupage medium. Let them dry.

Leading Eggs

Bold, geometric designs are made even more graphic with the addition of dimensional leading.

- 2 shades of acrylic paint
- Clear acrylic matte spray varnish
- Liquid leading

1. Paint eggs with one shade of acrylic paint. Let the paint dry completely.
2. Paint simple geometric designs onto the egg with the second shade of paint. Let the painted designs dry.
3. Spray the painted eggs with the acrylic varnish. Allow the varnished eggs to dry overnight.
4. Outline the painted geometric shapes with the liquid leading. Work on half of an egg at a time. Allow the leading to dry before finishing the egg.

Anaconda Eggs

No, not the snakes! They don't lay their eggs in copper nests. These are named after the great 20th-century copper mining company.

- Copper foil tape
- Decorative paper punches
- Bone folder

1. Cut thin strips of copper tape with scissors or decorative-edge scissors. Use the decorative paper punches to punch out shapes from the foil tape. Set the strips and shapes to the side.

2. Peel off the paper backing from a strip or shape. Place it on the egg as desired. Use a gentle, even pressure to rub the foil with the bone folder. This will burnish the foil and remove any wrinkles or folds. Don't fret: You'll have to exert a lot of pressure to crack the shell.

Blue Willow

Prettily printed paper napkins are the perfect material to decoupage onto delicate eggshells. The only difficulty will be choosing which pattern to use: there are so many napkins out there!

- Decorative paper napkins
- Decoupage medium

1. Cut out the design elements from the napkin you have chosen.

2. Carefully peel apart the layers of the cut-out elements. Sometimes this process is a bit tricky, and you'll probably tear some of the elements. Don't fret: You bought a whole pack of napkins anyway, didn't you? Set the top, colored layer to one side. Cut out more design elements than you think you'll need for your project.

3. Brush a thin coat of decoupage glue onto the area of the egg that you want to cover. Carefully position one of the design elements onto the egg. Use your clean fingertips to pat the napkin onto the egg.

4. Continue adding design elements to the eggs. You may find it easier to allow a glued area to dry before adding more elements.

5. When you like the appearance of an egg, let it dry completely. Coat the entire egg with a final coat of decoupage medium for protection.

Fiber Eggs

This project gives you a good excuse to buy even more colorful and fanciful fibers. Simply wrap eggs with your favorite fibers, and add the leftovers (if you have any) to your crafter's stash.

- Perle cottons, embroidery floss, and decorative yarns
- Thick, white craft glue

1. Use a small dab of glue to anchor the end of a length of yarn or thread in place.
2. Wind and wrap your thread around the egg. Use small dabs of glue to attach the thread to the shell as you go. If you don't glue as you go, you may find yourself with an unraveling egg or a stripe than won't neatly stay in place. Follow the directions on page 18 to secure your glued fibers to the egg until they're dry.
3. Cut your thread and anchor the end with a dab of glue. If desired, wrap contrasting textures or colors around the egg. You can create interesting effects by wrapping with two or more types of thread.
4. To create a whorl or spiral, use a pin or toothpick to hold the glued end of thread in place as you wrap it round and round.

Trim Eggs

Rows of ribbon, beautiful braids, beaded cords, or woven trims can all be used to great effect on eggs.

- 2 yards (1.8 m) of decorative cord per egg*
- Decorative ribbon
- Rickrack
- Hot glue

*You'll need this much cord to create the eggs as shown on the right.

1. To completely cover an egg (as shown on the right) start on the bottom of the egg. Place a dot of hot glue on the egg. Attach the end of the cord to the glue.

2. Place tiny dots of hot glue around the first glued down section, and coil the cord around the starting point. Continue to work around the egg, adding a small amount of glue, then adhering the trim to the egg until you reach the point of the egg. Don't be tempted to just slather glue on the egg before wrapping the cord—you'll be disappointed in the results.

3. To wrap an egg with ribbon or rickrack, simply measure the egg (page 16) and adhere either to the egg with the glue of your choice.

Shibori Eggs

Soft, blurry-edged patterns are one of the charms of this adaptation of the Japanese dyeing technique known as shibori.

- Dyes
- Rubber bands, stickers, or tape

1. Prepare the dye you have chosen. If it needs to cool before using, prepare the dye ahead of time.
2. Unblown or hard cooked eggs work best for this process. Both sink in the dye bath, so they don't have to be held down.
3. Rubber bands wraipped around eggs yield excellent, strong-patterned linear resists. Other good resists are stickers in simple shapes, yarns and string, and freehand shapes cut from masking tape.
4. Submerge eggs in the prepared dye for five to 10 minutes.
5. Remove eggs from the dye solution with a slotted spoon. Place the eggs on a drying rack if you have one and allow them to dry completely before removing the resists.
6. You may repeat the resist and dyeing process with a different dye color to create more complex patterns.
7. If desired, blow the eggs following the directions on page 10.

Peeps

*These charmingly painted little "peeps"
are easier to create than you think.*

- Yellow, white, red, black or
  blue gouache paint*
- Fine-tipped brush

*Gouache paints are opaque watercolors. Substitute
acrylic paints if you wish.*

1. Use a pencil to lightly sketch the outline of
   the chick onto the egg.

2. Mix your paints to create the pale yellow,
   white, rose, and blue used on these eggs. The
   delicate colors of gouache work best when
   applied in layers to achieve a soft, opaque
   effect. Paint in the base color of pale yellow
   on top of your pencil sketch and let it dry.
   Apply additional coats to achieve a more
   intense color as desired.

3. To give the chick more definition, use the rosy
   color to define feet, beak, and wing, and to
   outline the shape of the little bird. Add
   touches of white to highlight the chick if
   desired. Add an eye created with a simple,
   very dark blue dot.

Pearl Eggs

Pearls—symbols of purity like the egg itself—
were once the most prized of the ancient
gemstones. It would cost a maharajah's ransom
to lavishly pave eggs with pearls, so here's
the next best thing.

- Prestrung craft "pearls"
- Hot glue

1. Place a small amount of hot glue on the bottom of the egg. Immediately adhere the end of the bead string to the egg.
2. Add dots of glue in a circle around the first bead, and coil the bead string around the first bead.
3. Continue to wrap the bead string around the egg, adding a small amount of glue as needed. Don't attempt to glue more than a little bit at a time.
4. If you wish to use more than one color, just trim the strung beads at the place where you want the color to end. Start the next color right up against the first.
5. Continue gluing and placing beads as needed until you reach the top of the egg.

Guest Designer: Joan Morris

High Tech Eggs & Baskets

These baskets are an out-of-the-ordinary way to present special eggs. Sew them together with colored wire if you wish and add embossed metal tags with the recipients' names and the date.

- ¹/4-inch (6mm) hardware cloth
- 22-gauge wire
- Wire snips
- Pliers
- Flat or half round file
- Scrap of 2x4 lumber
- Wooden dowel
- Twist ties*

* Use these to temporarily wire together the basket while you "sew" up the sides.

1. Decide what size of basket you want. A 4-inch square (10.2 x10.2 cm) basket is a good size for a large, single egg.

2. Measure, mark, and cut out an 4-inch square (10.2 x10.2 cm) of paper.

3. Cut a length of hardware cloth three times longer than the square you have cut out of paper. Use wire snips or shears to cut this length from the roll. Gently press it with your hands until it's flat.

4. Center your pattern on the hardware cloth and tape it down.

5. You are going to cut out four corners to create a cross shape. It's easy to make this cross accurate. Cut one section at a time. Start and cut from one edge to the corner of the paper square. Then rotate the hardware cloth to make a similar cut to the corner.

6. When all four corners have been removed, go back along the edges with wire cutters and cut off the burrs created as you cut. Use a flat file to gently file the edges for a smooth finish.

7. Using the scrap of 2x4 as an edge, you are going to "upset" the sides of the basket. Gently fold up the sides one at time.

8. How tall do you want the sides of your basket to be? Do you want a straight edge or a

rolled edge? For a straight edge, simply decide how tall you want the sides, and then trim the hardware cloth. For a rolled edge, place a length of dowel along the top edge of one side and gently roll the edge down as desired. You can now temporarily wire the corners together with the twist ties.

9. Cut a length of wire about twice as long as the desired height of the basket sides.

10. Working from the bottom of the basket, join two sides by twisting one end of the wire on itself.

11. Use the wire much in the same way you would use thread. Whipstitch evenly up the side. Stitch every square or every other square. Use your pliers to tighten the stitches as you go along.

12. Whipstitch up to the desired height. Leave the end of the wire free.

13. Whipstitch each of the remaining sides, leaving the ends of wire free.

14. Use the free ends of the wire to whip stitch rolled edges to the basket. Otherwise, simply wrap the wire around one of the hardware cloth wires a couple of times and snip it off.

15. Finish all edges in this manner.

16. Cut a length of hardware cloth for a handle. File the edges until smooth. Whipstitch the handle to the basket with wire.

For the Eggs

- Silver composition leaf
- Colored tacks

1. Follow the directions on page 52 for gilding eggs.

2. Hammer colorful tacks in rows or other patterns on the eggs.

Rhinestone Eggs

They're not Fabergé,
but these jeweled eggs look
like a million bucks!

- Tweezers
- Cyanoacrylate glue
- Acrylic jewels and rhinestones

1. You'll need the tweezers to pick up and place each individual jewel.
2. Put a small dot of glue on an egg and place a rhinestone on it. Place your jewels randomly or create patterns: Simple bands, crosses, and flowerlike designs are easiest to do.

Ooops! Mosaics

Don't throw them in the compost pile!
Don't float them in the coffee pot!
Save those eggshells for mosaics.

- Dyes
- Small containers
- White craft glue
- Straight pin or sewing needle

1. You've dropped an egg on the counter or you've blown too hard and the egg has—so to speak—left you with you-know-what all over your face. Save those shells!

2. Dye broken shells and whole eggs in variety of colors. Let the dyed eggs dry.

3. Crumble the broken shells into very small pieces (very cathartic). Crack the whole eggs (or peel them if they're hard-cooked) and crumble them as well. Have small containers handy to sort the different colors.

4. Lightly sketch designs on unbroken eggs. They may be dyed or left in their natural state.

5. Fill a small portion of the design with small amount of craft glue. Dip the point of a pin or needle in craft glue. Then use the point to pick up a piece of shell. Place the fragment on the glue within the design. Continue this process until the design is filled.

6. You can use large fragments to decorate eggs in a free-form mosaic style.

Guest Designer: Lynne Caldwell

Springtime Blooms

These lighthearted eggs—with all the frills upon them—are as pretty and fanciful as the hats in the Easter parade.

- Polystyrene foam eggs
- 3 to 4 silk flowers per egg*
- Hot glue

Marigolds, zinnias, and hyacinths were used on these eggs. When using hyacinths, simply pull the small blooms from the flower head and glue them onto the egg.

1. Disassemble a flower head by cutting the stem close to the bottom of the flower. Carefully remove the petals from the stem. Try to keep the petals in order as you remove them.

2. Glue the bottom layer of petals from the flower head on the wide bottom of the egg.

3. Pick up the next layer of petals and cut the petals into smaller sections. Glue one section at a time to the egg, slipping the section underneath the previous row. Layer the petals around the egg until the egg is completely covered.

4. Finish the egg by gluing two or three leaves to the large end of the egg.

The Goose Laid These

Some of these aren't golden, but they're all gilded.

- Wooden eggs*
- Red and blue acrylic paints
- Composition leaf (gold, copper, variegated, and silver)
- Adhesive size
- Square of soft cloth
- Clear acrylic varnish
- Costume jewelry, upholstery tacks (optional)

* You can gild any type of egg. Wooden eggs are used in this project. Old costume jewelry was attatched to some of the eggs with strong glue or small nails before they were gilded. Decorative upholstery tacks were hammered into one of the eggs.

1. Give each egg a base coat of acrylic paint. Red paint looks best under the gold, copper, and variegated leaf; blue paint, under silver. Let the paint dry.
2. Work on half of an egg at a time. Coat each half with adhesive size. Follow the manufacturer's instructions for drying time.
3. Pick up a small amount of leaf and apply it to the egg. Smooth down the leaf with the soft cloth.
4. Coat the second half with adhesive size. Apply the leaf when the size is ready.
5. Coat the gilded egg with acrylic varnish to protect the leaf from tarnishing.

Etched Eggs

Brush up on your rudimentary knowledge of chemistry. Do you remember that vinegar is an acid and not a salt or a base (whatever that means)? Use this kitchen-cabinet acid to etch simple designs on eggshells.

- Whole eggs
- Beeswax
- Kistka or tjanting tool
- White vinegar
- Glass container
- Spoon
- Rubber gloves

1. Use unblown or hard-cooked brown, green, or other naturally colored eggs for this project.

2. Follow the manufacturer's instructions for using a kistka or tjanting tool. Use the tool to paint designs onto an egg with hot wax. Keep in mind that the egg's color will be removed around the area where the wax has been painted.

3. Submerge the egg in a container of white vinegar. You may need to add more vinegar to the container so that the egg is completely covered. Turn the egg with a spoon to ensure that the egg is evenly etched. Leave the egg in the vinegar for at least five minutes and up to 20 minutes. The longer the egg is in the vinegar, the deeper the etched effect.

4. Remove the egg from the vinegar. Wearing rubber gloves hold the egg under hot running water to rinse the egg and remove the wax.

5. Blow the egg, if desired, following the instructions on page 10.

Bead Netting Eggs

Bead netting creates a simple, graphic effect on white eggs.

- Beading thread*
- Size 10 beading needle
- Seed beads, size 11/0
- Cyanoacrylate glue (optional)

* If you've chosen to bead with dark beads, use a dark beading thread. Use a white thread if you're using light-colored beads.

Capped Chicken Egg

1. Thread the needle with about 2 yards (1.8 m) of beading thread. Double the thread to give it strength.

2. Put one of the seed beads on the thread. Bring it to the end of thread, leaving a 6-inch (15 cm) tail. Go back through the bead, making a loop around it to hold it in place.

3. String 10 more beads. Go back through the first bead you strung, creating a loop. Thread the needle through the next seven beads.

4. Add eight beads to the thread. Pass the needle through the three beads on the side of the loop, so there are two beads on the top, three on each side, and three on the bottom.

5. Thread the needle through the three beads on the bottom of the loop you just made, then through the three beads on the side.

6. Repeat steps 4 and 5 until you've made a chain of bead loops long enough to go around the top of the egg.

7. To close the chain, add the two beads that go on the top of the loop. Thread through the three beads on the side of the first loop of the chain. Add the three bottom beads and thread through the three beads on the side of the last loop in the chain.

8. Tie off the thread and weave it through several of the beads before cutting it. Tie off the tail from step 2 in the same way.

9. Slip the netted bands onto the egg. If needed, secure the band permanently to the egg with a dab of cyanoacrylate glue.

Triangle Net Chain

1. Thread the needle with about 2 yards (1.8 m) of the dark blue beading thread. Double the thread to give it strength.

2. Put one of the seed beads on the thread. Bring it to the end of thread, leaving a 6-inch tail. Go back through the bead, making a loop around it to hold it in place.

3. Add 19 more beads and pass through the first bead you put on, creating a loop.

4. Thread the needle through the next five beads in the loop. Add 15 more beads and pass back through the five beads that will make the side of the loop.

5. Repeat step 4 until you've made a chain long enough to go around the middle of the egg.

6. To close the chain, add five beads, pass through five beads on the side of the first loop you created, add five more beads, and pass through the five beads on the side of the last loop you created.

7. Tie off the thread and weave it through several of the beads before cutting it. Tie off the tail from step 2 in the same way.

8. Slip the netted band onto the egg. If needed, secure the band permanently to the egg with a dab of cyanoacrylate glue.

Square Net Chain

1. Thread the needle with about 2 yards (1.8 m) of the dark blue beading thread. Double the thread to give it strength.

2. Put one of the seed beads on the thread. Bring it to the end of thread, leaving a 6-inch tail. Go back through the bead, making a loop around it to hold it in place.

3. Add 27 beads and pass through the first bead you put on, creating a loop. Thread the needle through 20 of the beads on the loop. Each side will have seven beads.

4. Add 21 more beads and thread the needle through the seven beads on the side of the first loop. Go through 14 of the beads on that loop, so your thread exits at the top or bottom of one of the sides.

5. Repeat step 4 until you have a chain long enough to go around the middle of the egg.

6. To close off the chain, add seven beads for the top of the loop and pass through the seven beads on the side of the first loop you created. Add seven beads for the bottom of the loop and pass through the seven beads on the side of the last loop you created.

7. Tie off the thread and weave it through several of the beads before cutting it. Tie off the tail from step 2 in the same way.

8. Slip the netted band onto the egg. If needed, secure the band permanently to the egg with a dab of cyanoacrylate glue.

Sticker Eggs

Big, bright, and bold results. Really fast. Really easy.

- Plastic eggs
- Stickers

1. The hardest task in the project is choosing what stickers you'll want to use. Be forewarned; there's a huge array of stickers to choose from.

2. Peel and stick. Really, it's that easy.

3. Pile the eggs in a brightly colored bowl.

Pop Art Eggs

These dramatic sculptural eggs are worth the time and effort it takes to create them.

- Blown eggs with a single hole*
- Small syringe
- Dye
- Modeling clay
- Circle templates
- Hand-held, motorized cutting tool
- Conical burr
- Dust mask
- Safety glasses

Goose eggs and ostrich eggs (they both have hard shells) are easiest to work on. If you're so inclined try regular hen's eggs, but be forewarned that their delicate shells require a practiced, deft touch.

1. Fill the syringe with dye. Inject the dye into the egg's single hole. You'll need to repeat this process several times to ensure you have enough dye to color the inside of the egg.

2. Pinch off a piece of modeling clay. Plug the hole with the clay.

3. Gently shake and rotate the egg to make isure you have the interior dyed as evenly as possible.

4. Remove the clay and allow the dye to drip out. You'll need to set the egg on a drying rack (page 13) at least overnight.

5. Use the templates and a pencil to draw different sized holes on the egg.

6. Fit a conical burr in the cutting tool.

7. Wear a dust mask and safety glasses as you drill a small hole in the center of each drawn circle. Enlarge each circle further with the burr.

Bas Relief Eggs

Spackling paste? Really? What charming results from such a prosaic material.

- Acrylic paints
- Spackling paste
- Small scale plastic stencils
- Craft sticks
- Plastic pastry bag and tips (optional)
- Clear matte acrylic spray

1. Paint eggs with acrylics and let them dry.

2. Place a stencil on an egg, carefully wrapping it around the egg if needed. You can hold the stencil in place with tape if needed.

3. Scoop up a small amount of spackling paste with a craft stick and wipe it evenly onto the stencil. Because the egg is rounded, you may have to apply the spackling paste in stages, letting each section dry before applying more paste.

4. Carefully remove stencil.

5. If you wish to make colored spackling paste, simply mix a tiny amount of acrylic paint to the paste until you achieve the color you desire.

6. A more dimensional look can be achieved by filling a pastry bag fitted with a star tip with the spackling paste. Follow the manufacturer's instructions for using the pastry bag, and apply the paste to the egg creating a small flower shape.

7. When dry, coat the eggs with the clear acrylic spray.

Flower Garden Eggs

How does your garden grow? The charming bouquets on these eggs were meant to decorate scrapbook pages.

- Paper scrapbook embellishments
- White craft glue
- Pale green vellum
- Terra-cotta pots
- Paper shredder (optional)

1. Trim the flowers as needed. Adhere the flowers to the eggs with small amounts of glue.
2. Cut 1-inch (2.54 cm) by 11-inch (27.9 cm) strips of vellum. Trim them as needed to fit inside the circumference of each pot.
3. Cut thin slits along the length of each strip of vellum to create blades of grass.
4. Glue the grass to the interior edge of each pot.
5. Create your own matching grass by running vellum through a paper shredder. Place the grass in each pot to support the egg.
6. Plant an egg in each pot.

Humpty Dumpty Candles

Uh-oh. Don't throw them away. Here's what you can do with those broken eggshells.

- Dye
- Wicks
- Wax or candle ends
- Clean tin can
- Pan
- Egg carton
- Spoon

1. Dye your broken eggshells, if they aren't already colored.
2. Cut short lengths of wick, long enough fit inside the shell.
3. Melt wax (or even short lengths of candles) on the stove in a clean tin can set in a pot of water.
4. Set the broken shells in an egg carton. Carefully spoon wax into each shell to anchor the wick. Then fill the shell to just below the broken edge with wax. Let the wax cool and harden.
5. Set the candles in egg cups before you light them. Never leave a burning egg (candle) unattended.

Shells

Oh, the irony of the embellishment!

- Craft shells
- Hot glue

1. Use the tiniest shells you can find.
2. One at a time, hot glue each shell to an egg.
3. Bands made of shells are easy to do. Overlap them slightly if needed. If you have a special shell saved from a summer vacation, use it as a focal embellishment. The tiny sand dollars were carefully preserved from a trip to the Gulf Coast.

Toile de Jouy Lapin

This French hare skips lightly over the arcadian landscape with his egg-filled basket. Perhaps he's on his way to a springtime frolic?

- Papier mâché egg
- White acrylic paint or gesso
- Patterned tissue paper
- Decoupage medium
- Black tissue paper
- Hare template
- Stapler
- Wire-edge ribbon

1. Brush a coat of acrylic paint or gesso on the egg. Let it dry.

2. Follow the directions on page 17 for covering an egg with paper. Apply the tissue paper to the egg with decoupage medium and let it dry.

3. Photocopy the hare template. Enlarge or reduce the template as needed. Lay the photocopy on several layers of black tissue and staple them all together. Cut out the silhouette of the hare.

4. Coat an area of the egg equal to the size of the hare silhouette. Carefully place the hare on the egg, smoothing out the tissue with your fingers. Let the tissue dry.

5. Give the egg a coat of decoupage medium.

6. Cut small holes in the eggs at the top and bottom. Thread a doubled length of ribbon through the egg to create a hanger. Knot the ribbon at the bottom of the egg to hold the loop in place. Create a simple bow with matching ribbon and tie it to the looped end.

Hydrangea Eggs

Dried blossoms from the flower heads of oak-leaf hydrangea are a perfectly delicate accent for pale brown eggs.

- Dried hydrangea blossoms
- Seam binding
- White craft glue
- Nests
- Rustic napkin rings

1. Harvest dried oak-leaf hydrangea blossoms from your garden. You can also find other varieties of dried hydrangeas in florist shops and craft stores.
2. Trim the stem from each individual blossom on the back side of the flower. Set them to the side.
3. Wrap seam binding around each egg as desired. Secure the seam binding with tiny dabs of glue.
4. Place a dab of glue on the back of each blossom. Place the blossoms on the eggs as desired.
5. Nestle eggs in man-made nests and perch them on rustic twig napkin rings.

Batik Eggs

The sophisticated look of batik is easy to achieve.
You use hot wax to draw simple patterns right on the egg.

- *Kistky* or *tjanting* tool (page 13)
- Beeswax
- Dyes*
- Paper towels
- Microwave oven

*Dyes that are to be used cool, rather than hot, are a must for this project.
A lukewarm or hot dye bath will melt the wax resist.

1. Start with naturally colored or lightly dyed eggs. Unblown or hard-cooked eggs will be easier to dye than blown eggs.

2. You may wish to sketch your designs onto the eggs ahead of time, but the pencil marks may not disappear as you dye the eggs. Instead of sketching complex designs directly on an egg, use stripes, geometric shapes, or simple drawings for your first attempts at batik.

3. Follow the manufacturer's instructions for using your kistky or tjanting tool. You will be drawing with liquid wax on the eggshell. This is accomplished by heating small amounts of wax in the tool and drawing the tip of the tool across the surface of the shell. You may wish to practice with the tool on paper to get a feel for the process.

4. You'll discover that the liquid wax hardens almost instantly, so you won't have to wait long before you can dye the eggs. Submerge eggs into a cool dye bath and carefully turn them to ensure even coloring and to prevent your waxed design from chipping off.

5. Allow your dyed eggs to dry, then repeat the waxing and dyeing process as many times as you'd like. Just remember to begin the dyeing process with very light colors, moving to darker colors each time you redye. Each time you wax a design on the egg you will preserve the color underneath the wax.

6. Blow each egg when you are finished with your design (page 10).

7. Place an egg on a paper towel in the microwave oven. Heat the egg for five to 15 seconds. Remove the egg and immediately rub off the wax with a paper towel. Repeat as many times as needed to remove the wax.

Guest Designer: Lynne Caldwell

Alien Eggs

Alien eggs? Use tiny wiggly craft eyes for an entirely different and other-worldly look.

- Tiny craft pompoms
- White craft glue
- A steady hand

1. Put a dab of glue on a pompom.
2. With a steady hand, cover the surface of each egg with pompoms.

White-on-White Eggs

Who knew that a quick survey of the bridal and millinery aisle of your local craft store could yield such elegant eggs? Mind you: Clean hands and fingers are a must for this project.

- Bridal and millinery trimmings
- Thick, white craft glue
- Hot glue

1. Measure your eggs (page 16). Doing so helps you cut your materials with less waste. After all, you've a lot of eggs to trim.

2. Apply small dots of glue to the back of the trimming you've chosen. Carefully apply the trimming to the egg with gentle pressure. If needed, follow the directions on page 18 to hold the trim in place while the glue dries.

3. Cut apart any wired trims such as flowers or leaves. You can twist two or three leaves together, slip the twisted stems into the hole you've made to blow the egg, and secure the stems with hot glue. Use hot glue to attach the leaf tips to the egg.

Chinoiserie Eggs

Definitely Chinese influenced.
Most certainly elegant.

- Red and black acrylic paints
- Chinese theme rubber stamps
- Gold ink pad
- Oriental papers
  (joss papers, foreign language newspapers)
- Decoupage medium
- Gold paint pen
- High-gloss, clear acrylic spray

1. Paint the eggs red or black. Let them dry.
2. Carefully stamp images onto the eggs with gold ink. Let the stamped images dry.
3. Cut out small shapes from the Oriental papers. Brush a thin coat of decoupage medium onto a shape and apply it to the egg. Apply additional shapes, overlapping them as desired. Set the egg aside to dry.
4. Outline the shapes with the gold paint pen. You can also paint additional shapes onto the egg. Let the paint dry.
5. Spray the egg with high-gloss clear spray and let it dry.

Painter's Frenzy

Why settle for using just one technique per egg? Play with patterns and painting techniques until you run out of shell space.

- Wooden eggs
- Acrylic paints
- Gesso
- Acrylic modeling paste
- Craft stick
- Masking tape
- Sea sponge
- Acrylic varnish

1. Give each egg a base coat of white paint or gesso. Let them dry.

2. To create the textured band on the largest egg, the designer masked off a stripe around the egg with tape. Use a craft stick to spread a thick coat of modeling paste to the masked off section. Texture, texturing it as you go. Set the egg aside and let the modeling paste dry overnight. Remove the tape and you'll have a textured band with crisp edges. Paint or gild the band.

3. The mottled background on the eggs was created with several colors of paint and a sea sponge. First, give the egg a base coat of color and then sponge contrasting colors on top.

4. Mask off shapes on the egg. Give them a coat of paint.

5. Outline the shapes with dozens of dots. Create the dots with the end of a paint brush dipped in paint. Layer dots on top of each other in different colors for a slightly dimensional effect.

6. Add comma shapes to the surfaces with a pointed paint brush. They're easy to do.

7. Finish each egg with a coat of acrylic varnish.

Bunny Portraits

No two bunnies look alike, so don't be afraid to create these bunny portraits. Start with a simple shape and add the details as you go.

- Brown, white, yellow, black, and red gouache*
- Fine-point paintbrush

*Use acrylic paints if you wish.

1. Lightly sketch the outline of the bunny head onto the egg. Paint it brown. Let it dry.
2. Mix a bit of black with the brown. Paint the eye shape on the head.
3. Paint three small white circles at the tip of the bunny's head to create the nose and mouth area.
4. Mix brown, white, and yellow. Highlight the bunny's eye and nose areas.
5. Use a dark brown color to add eyelashes, whiskers, the nose line, and a small mouth.
6. Add a tiny dot of white in each eye to make it sparkle.
7. Mix red and white to create a soft pink. Paint the pink on the ears.

Guest Designer: Susan McBride

Polymer Clay Coils

Faux ivory, jade, and coral are created with mixtures of polymer clay to adorn these eggs.

- Blown eggs
- White, translucent, gold, green pearl, and alizarin crimson polymer clay*
- Waxed paper
- Burnt umber acrylic paint
- Cotton cloth
- Water
- Cyanoacrylate glue gel
- Polymer clay compatible glaze (optional)
- Clay gun
- Craft knife
- Needle tool or awl
- Pasta machine (optional)

Please follow general safety instructions for polymer clay. Kitchen tools used for these projects (e.g., pasta machine or rolling pin) should be solely dedicated for use with polymer clay. Protect your work surface with waxed paper. Condition clay before use by kneading and rolling it in your hands or by running it several times through a pasta machine at the thickest setting.

Mixing the Clay

For the ivory egg, use conditioned white clay.

To achieve the color for the jade eggs, mix pea-size balls of pearl green and gold together. Condition one bar of translucent clay, then mix in small amounts of the green pearl and gold mixture until the desired color is achieved.

Mix a very small amount of alizarin crimson clay with one bar of conditioned translucent clay for coral. The crimson is a very strong color, so start with less than you think you need. You can always add more crimson if desired.

General Instructions

1. Fit a disc with a round opening in the clay gun.

2. Roll the conditioned, colored clay into a log that will fit in the clay gun.

3. Insert the plunger into the barrel of the clay gun and push. Holding the clay gun over the wax paper, direct the emerging ropes of clay back and forth so that they don't overlap.

4. Pick up one end of the extruded rope and roll the rope into a tight flat spiral. When the spiral is the size of a small coin, position it on one end of the egg. Press into place, then continue coiling the clay around the egg. Make sure each new row touches the previous and that the clay is pressed snugly against the egg.

5. When the desired amount of the egg is covered, cut the clay rope and press the end firmly on the egg.

6. To make spirals of equal size use uniform lengths of clay.

7. Fill in spaces on the egg with short, cut lengths of rope. Fit them into open spaces on the egg. Trim as needed, then press the pieces firmly onto the egg.

8. You can create dots by cutting very short lengths of rope and rolling each length between your fingertips to create a small ball. Gently position them on the egg and press into place. If desired, the end of a paintbrush may be pressed into the balls of clay after they are in place to create a dimpled dot.

9. When the egg is covered, use a needle tool or awl to open a small hole in the clay which may be covering the hole. This will allow any steam resulting from moisture that's still inside the egg to escape during baking rather than damaging the egg.

10. Bake the clay-covered egg, following the manufacturers instructions for the brand of clay you are using.

11. When cool, apply a generous amount of the burnt umber acrylic paint to the polymer clay. Immediately begin wiping away excess with a soft cotton cloth to create an antiqued finish. Moisten the cloth with water for a lighter finish, if desired.

12. If a portion of the clay is not securely adhered to the egg you may need to secure the loose element with a small dot of cyanoacrylate glue. Hold the element in place for several seconds until glue is set.

13. For a glossy finish, brush on a coat of glaze.

Vintage Ostrich Egg

Images from vintage Easter postcards make charming egg embellishments.

- Postcard
- Water release transfer paper
- Hair dryer

1. Search antique stores, flea markets, and online for collectible Easter postcards. You'll find lots of chicks and bunnies to choose from.
2. Follow the manufacturer's instructions for transferring the image to the paper.
3. Follow the manufacturer's instructions for applying the transfer paper to a curved surface. You'll find that using a hair dryer will help the transfer conform to the curved surface of the egg.

Ormolu Eggs

Ormolu is not an animal. It's the gilded brass decorations found on Louis-the-Something-or-Other furniture. Imagine a beribboned Marie Antoinette and her courtiers hunting for these eggs in the gardens of Versailles.

- Acrylic paints
- Gold paper doilies
- Glue stick
- Decoupage medium

1. Paint your eggs in the colors of your choice. Set the eggs aside to dry.
2. Peel apart the layers of the doilies.
3. Cut out the sections of the doily you wish to use.
4. Coat the back of the doily section with the glue stick. Place the doily on the egg, patting it in place with your finger. Cover the egg as desired. If the doily sections don't stick, follow the instructions on how to glue almost anything to an egg on page 18.
5. When dry, coat the entire egg with decoupage medium.

Guest Designer: Joan Morris

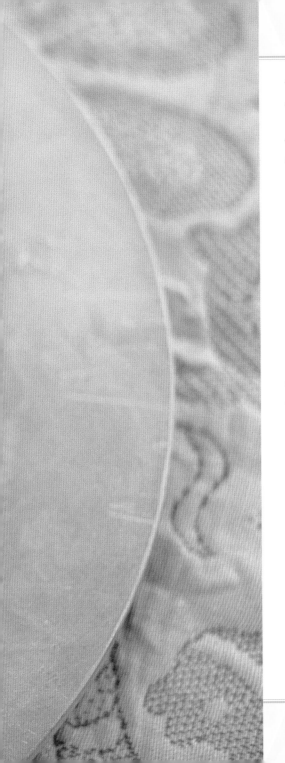

Mehndi Eggs

Intricate patterning and delicately stencilled designs are hallmarks of the Indian art of mehndi, or henna painting.

- Mehndi stencils*
- Acrylic paints
- Small stencil brush
- Newspaper

*These flexible stencils can be found online, in specialty shops, and in many Asian markets. They cling to the curved surface of an eggshell quite well.

1. Color some eggs with dye or acrylic paint. You may leave eggs uncolored if you wish.

2. Lay a stencil onto a colored or uncolored egg.

3. Pour out a small amount of paint onto a piece of paper. Lightly dip the stencil brush in the paint, then pounce the brush on newspaper until a light coat of paint is left on the paper. If the brush is loaded with too much paint, the stencil design won't have crisp edges when you stencil the egg.

4. Gently pounce paint onto the stencil. Take care that the stencil does not shift. Pick up additional paint on your brush, pounce it, and add more color on the egg if needed. Let the paint dry for a bit before you remove the stencil.

Visually Pun-y Eggs

Whatever you do, don't restrain yourself! Puns can be as silly or risqué as you wish. Here are some of obvious choices; imagine what you can do if you let yourself go.

- Clip art
- Wet release transfer paper*
- Portable hair dryer
- Shadowbox frame

*You'll find wet release transfer in most craft stores. It's sometimes referred to as water-slide decal paper. Some transfer papers require color photocopying to finish the decal; others can be used with inkjet printers.

1. Search for egg related clip art in books and on the Internet. Print out the images you find amusing.

2. Enlarge or reduce the images as needed.

3. Follow the manufacturer's instructions for copying onto the transfer paper.

4. Carefully cut out the image you wish to use.

5. To adhere the transfer paper, you soak the cut out image in a container of water and then slide it onto the surface you wish to place the image on. Follow the specific instructions for the paper you are using.

6. Once the image is on the egg, you can ease wrinkles onto the curved surface by gently heating the decal with a hair dryer. Let the image dry.

7. Display your eggs with style. We placed one egg in a shadowbox on a printed paper that mimics antique writing. Another egg was showcased under a glass dome.

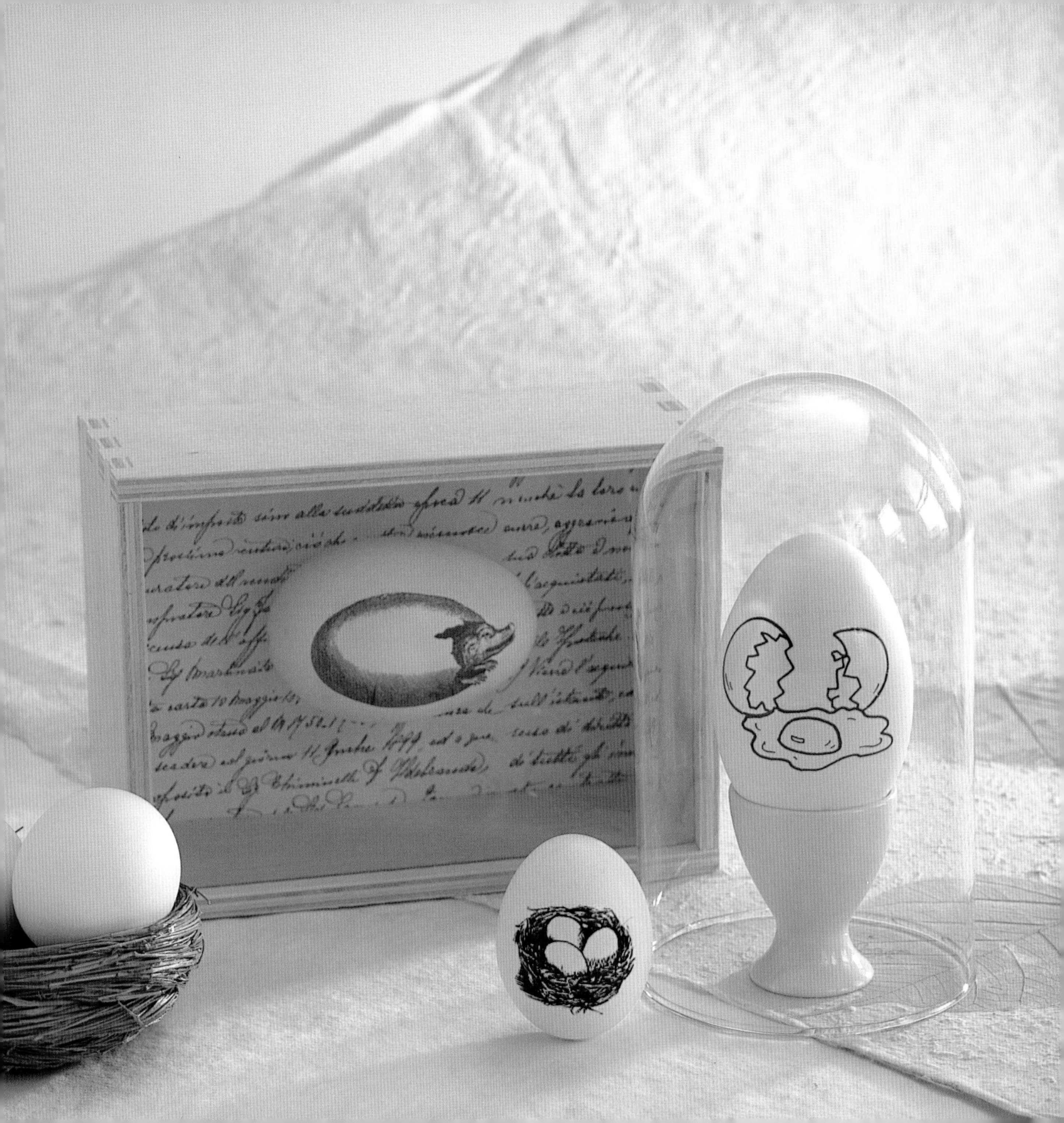

Pyrographic Pysanky

Woodburned dots create the starlike patterns and other simple shapes on these eggs. They may not be as colorful as their pysanky cousins, but the intricate patterning echoes the Ukrainian flair for precise decoration.

- Scrap wood*
- Wooden eggs
- Woodburning tool with circle and fine all-purpose points*
- Fine-grit sandpaper

*If you haven't tried woodburning since your camp days, you may wish to practice on a piece of scrap wood before starting to work on your eggs.

1. Divide an egg into quadrants (page 17). Lightly pencil the lines on the egg.

2. Sketch a pattern of your own on a piece of paper. If needed, sketch it directly on the egg. In traditional pysanky, star shapes represent success; sun shapes, the source of light and life. The circle—a shape with no beginning and no end—is one of the most powerful symbols for protection from evil.

3. Fit the fine all-purpose point into the woodburning tool. Preheat the tool following the manufacturer's directions.

4. Hold the tool perpendicular to the surface of the egg. Burn a small dot. It takes only a second or two to make a mark. Burn dots following your sketched pattern. Clean the point of the tool, occasionally scraping it lightly across the sandpaper.

5. When your designs are complete, erase any pencil lines.

Peachy Keen Baskets

Which came first, the basket or the eggs? Choose a tin can that has a label painted on the metal and make a unique basket. These baskets were made from peach cans, but yours might be made from a can of tomatoes or an exotic oriental sauce. Then, of course, match your eggs to the tin.

- Printed tin cans
- Solid-colored cookie tin
- Tin snips
- Work gloves
- Short length of wooden dowel
- Needle-nose pliers
- Awl
- Pop-rivet tool and rivets

1. Use the tin snips to make a small cut in the top wire rim of the printed can. Wearing work gloves, carefully removed the wire rim with the snips. Discard the wire rim.

2. Cut evenly spaced strips around the top of the can. If desired, you can trim the ends of the strips to form points.

3. Curl each strip around the wooden dowel or use pliers to curl each strip.

4. Create a handle for the basket by cutting a long, rectangular strip from the solid-colored tin. Use the awl to pierce each end.

5. Pierce one side of the can with the awl. Enlarge the hole for the rivet as needed.

6. Rivet one end of the handle to the inside of the basket. Pierce the opposite side of the can and rivet the other end of the handle.

For the Eggs

- Papier mâché eggs
- White acrylic paint or gesso
- Tissue papers
- Decoupage medium

1. Paint each egg with a coat of paint or gesso. Let them dry.

2. Tear one color of tissue paper into small squares. Apply overlapping squares to the egg with decoupage medium.

3. If desired, cut out circular shapes from contrasting tissue. The designer chose red to echo the colors of the peaches on the can. Adhere the shapes to the egg with decoupage medium. Let the egg dry.

4. Give each egg a finish coat of decoupage medium.

Foam Eggs

*Give the very youngest ones some bright craft-foam shapes
and let them work on unbreakable eggs.*

- Craft foam shapes*
- Plastic eggs
- White craft glue (optional)

*Purchase shapes with an adhesive backing if you find them.

1. Peel the backing from a shape or strip. Simply press it on the egg.

2. If you aren't using shapes with adhesive backing, brush a coat of glue on the back of each shape. Place it on the egg. Follow the directions on page 18 for holding anything on an egg.

Pique Assiette Eggs

Alas, these eggs are not particularly quick to make. You'll need at least two days to complete one (thanks to overnight drying time), but they're worth it. You'll save and display them for years to come.

- Variety of ceramic plates and saucers*
- Tile nippers
- Safety goggles or glasses
- Polystyrene foam egg or hard plastic egg
- Premixed tile mastic
- White sanded grout
- Acrylic paint (optional)
- Grout spreader and polyethylene foam wrap (white packing material)
- Mixing container for grout
- Palette knife
- Sponge and lint-free rags

You'll need more than you think, so buy 10 or 15 plates at thrift stores and yard sales.

1. Wearing goggles, prepare a supply of mosaic shards. Use tile nippers to break plates in half. Remove the rims from the plates. Trim the shards into small pieces. Set the pieces in a meat tray or other container. It is helpful to have several containers to separate the colors. Break the flat portions of the plate into small pieces.

2. Use the tile mastic to adhere small shards of pottery to the egg. Place them close together but not touching. Work on half of the egg, then let the egg sit for a few hours to dry.

3. Turn over the egg and finish attaching shards to it. Allow the mosaic to dry overnight before grouting.

4. Mix the white sanded grout according to manufacturer's instructions. If desired, add a small amount of acrylic paint to the mixture to color the grout.

5. Use a grout spreader or the polyethylene foam wrap to spread the grout over the surface of the mosaic. Use gentle pressure to force the grout into the spaces between the shards. After allowing the grout to set up for about 15 minutes, begin removing the excess grout with polyethylene foam wrap or clean, lint-free rags. Follow the manufacturer's recommendations on the grout for removing the grout haze that develops.

Bold Bumblebees

The first appearance of bumblebees in the garden is as much a harbinger of spring as the much-trumpeted bobbin' of the red, red robin.

- Black and yellow acrylic paints
- Acrylic spray varnish
- Black and white craft foam
- Yellow craft wire
- Hot glue
- Small craft eyes

1. Paint your eggs a bright shade of yellow. Let the paint dry, then paint black stripes on the eggs.
2. Once the paint is dry, give the eggs a coat of acrylic varnish.
3. Make wing shapes out of the white craft foam. Cut out two identical small circles of black craft foam for the head. Create a triangular-shape stinger with black foam.
4. Cut two short lengths of craft wire. Roll tiny coils on the ends to create the antennae.
5. Hot glue the antennae onto one of the head shapes. Sandwich the antennae between the two head pieces and glue the two circles together. Glue the eyes onto the head.
6. Attach the head, wings, and stinger onto the egg with hot glue.

Guest Designer: Joan Morris

Dots and Squiggles

Casual. Charming. Deceptively easy to do. Let your creativity run, jump, and skip while you paint whimsical designs.

- Gouaches*
- Colored pencils
- Clear acrylic spray fixative

Acrylic paints may also be used.

1. Hold an egg between your middle finger and thumb (or a craft lathe or bamboo skewer) while decorating it.

2. Gouache paints are opaque, matte colors that dry very quickly. Apply them liberally to each egg as a base coat. Let the base coat dry.

3. When the paint is dry, hold an egg in the palm of your hand and paint each end. Allow paint to dry.

4. Use a sharp pencil to lightly sketch designs onto eggs. Apply the gouache within the sketched designs. After the paint dries, outline the designs with a soft pencil or colored pencil.

5. Spray the finished eggs with fixative.

Guest Designer: Lynne Caldwell

Cracker Eggs

This colorful wrapping is reminiscent of crackers, the popping party favors that are a staple of British Christmas parties.

- Tissue paper
- Glue stick
- Narrow ribbon

1. Follow the directions on page 17 for covering an egg with paper. Make a rectangle twice as long as your longest measurement.
2. Cut out the rectangle of tissue paper.
3. Cut out a variety of geometric shapes, stripes, or other simple shapes from tissue of contrasting colors.
4. Attach the shapes to the rectangle with a glue stick. Press them under a heavy book until dry.
5. Wrap the decorated rectangle around the egg. Use narrow ribbon to tie each end. Flare out the edges with your fingers.

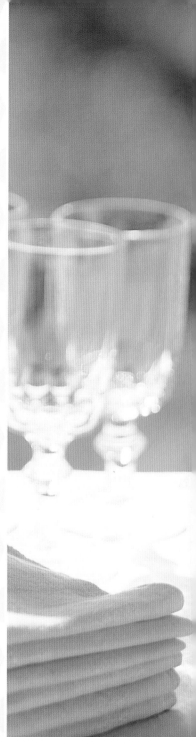

Artful Eggs in and around the Home

❧

An eggs-travaganza is the
one and only way to describe
this Easter buffet. Let us count
the ways. Suspend colorfully dyed
and blown eggs on purchased
wreath forms over the table, write
your guests' names on blown
eggs adorned with fine feathers,
use broken eggshells as serving
containers for sprouts, and
serve only egg-based
and egg-garnished dishes.

Here's an over-the-top
presentation for the
humble hard-cooked egg.
The extravagant ribbon
and organza ties serve no
functional purpose, so
they really say "fête"!

Smooth, white eggshells contrast with the vibrant flowers and greenery to
make an intriguing arrangement. Arrange blown or hard-cooked eggs around a block
of floral foam, then place dried or fresh flowers in the foam. Let your guests help
themselves to their own hard-cooked eggs from the boxes.

Create unusual and
memorable place settings
with place cards your guests
will demand to take home.
Transfer lettering—for the
name or an initial—is
perfect if you're not
comfortable with your own
handwriting on your
decorated (or plain) eggs.
Create your own tripods
with stems of dried
equisetum using a little hot
glue and raffia.

Stacked cake stands showcase a variety of hard-cooked eggs in this arrangement. The contrast of cotournix quail eggs (a common delicacy in Europe) with the more common brown and white chicken varieties gives your guests a tasty choice. Top off the arrangement with an egg-shaped candle.

An artful arrangement
of painted eggs paired
with fresh flowers and
lengths of ribbon is a
simple way to display your
creations. The colors of
the hand-painted bowl
echo the egg colors.

Ostrich eggs were once
rare curiosities proudly
displayed in Victorian
parlors. They're more
readily available these days
but still deserve to be
showcased. Casually placed
in worn terra-cotta pots,
they make a statement all
by themselves. When
paired with charming
cross-stitched samplers and
a relaxed arrangement
of spotted eggs, you get an
eye-catching display
that's bound to
elicit compliments.

If eggs can be artful,
they can certainly be
used in altered art.
Combine a purchased
box with a photocopied
bird image, dyed eggs,
and feathers from the
craft store to create a
mysterious homage to
your favorite bird.

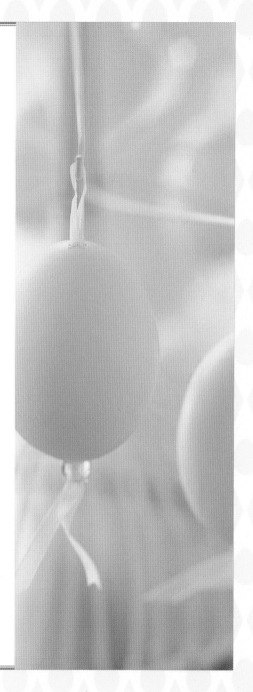

The oh-so-subtle varieties
of white in eggs of various sizes is
all you need to create an elegant
egg tree. Blow and clean the eggs,
then thread them on a doubled
length of ribbon with a simple
bead. Hang them on a wire tree or
a branch brought indoors.
This egg tree is destined to
be carefully packed away and
brought out again year
after year.

Wreaths are charming decorative accessories that are welcome in any room. The golden glow of an elegant lamp illuminates a diminutive commercially made wreath. Embellish the wreath with tiny quail eggs threaded onto silk ribbon, then hot glue the eggs to the form. A bold wall color is accented by the neutral tones of a grapevine wreath. Hot glue papier mâché eggs to a purchased wreath form and embellish it further with loosely tied raffia strands.

Guest Designer: Joan Morris

This unusual presentation of decorated eggs is a charming visual conceit
inspired by the story of coal miners carrying canaries into the mines. If the birds fell into
a faint (well, truly, if they died), the miners knew there was a gas leak, and skedaddled
out of the mine. Use clip art images copied onto a waterslide
transfer decal (page 92) to create the images.

Large plastic eggs covered with rich oriental papers (see page 17) are a
striking decorative accent any time of the year. Select papers to echo a color in the
room or in a painting, and place them in a contemporary basket.

Hanging colorful eggs in a springtime profusion of blossoms may be gilding the lily (so to speak), but it's charming in its own way. If you don't care for the idea of decorating an entire tree, why not bring a bare branch inside to bedeck with a few embellished eggs?

Who cares which
came first? (In truth,
it was the wire basket.)
Let an unusual object
put you on a creative
path that others fear to
tread. The soft pastel
eggs (what else would
you put in a wire hen?)
inspired the purchase
of a whimsical feather
boa from the craft
store. See what
happens when you let
your whims lead you?

If you can hang eggs
on trees, why not hang
them in a window?
Thread eggs and beads
on ribbon or monofilament
to create a jeweled scrim.
It's a cheerful addition
to the springtime view out
your window.

Guest Designer:
Lynne Caldwell

Guest Designers

Lynne Caldwell has a BA from the University of the South in Sewanee, Tennessee, and an MFA from Savannah College of Art and Design. She lives in Asheville, North Carolina, where she makes ikat weavings and teaches art to young children.

Susan Kieffer, the assistant editor of *FIBERARTS Magazine*, began experimenting with pyrography on a whim. Since then, several of her pyrographic projects have found their way into Lark publications.

Lynne Krucke's polymer clay creations have most recently appeared in *Faux Surfaces in Polymer Clay* (Lark, 2003). She's designed projects in card making, beading, rubber stamping, candles, and more for magazines and websites, as well as for several Lark books. She lives in Summerville, South Carolina, and can be contacted at lkrucke@bellsouth.net.

Susan McBride is much more than "just another art director" at Lark Books—she's a prolific artist and designer, as well as the proud mother of her own little "peep."

Joan Morris owns and operates Vincent's Ear, a coffee house and music venue in Asheville, North Carolina. In her spare time, she's created projects for several Lark books, including *Gifts for Baby* (2003), *Beautiful Ribbon Crafts* (2003), *Hardware Style* (2004). She's hard at work writing her first book for Lark, *The Weekend Crafter: Simple Upholstery* (2004).

Rain Newcomb lives in Asheville, North Carolina. During the day she works on Lark's series of books for children, and preserves her sanity by beading at night. She has been working with beads since she was 16, and despises making the same thing twice.

Karen Phillips is an avid crafter in many media. She's the seasonal manager for Ben Franklin Crafts in Asheville, North Carolina. She also displays and sells her original creations at The Screen Door in Asheville.

Index

A Note About Suppliers

Usually, the supplies you need for making the projects in Lark books can be found at your local craft supply store, discount mart, home improvement center, or retail shop relevant to the topic of the book. Occasionally, however, you may need to buy materials or tools from specialty suppliers. In order to provide you with the most up-to-date information, we have created a list of suppliers on our Web site, which we update on a regular basis. Visit us at www.larkbooks.com, click on "Craft Supply Sources," and then click on the relevant topic. You will find numerous companies listed with their web address and/or mailing address and phone number.